The Heisenberg Variations

Johns Hopkins: Poetry and Fiction
John T. Irwin, General Editor

JOHN BRICUTH

The
Heisenberg
Variations

The Johns Hopkins University Press
Baltimore and London

This book has been brought to publication with the
generous assistance of the Albert Dowling Trust.

Originally published by the University of Georgia Press
Johns Hopkins Paperbacks edition, 1988

The Johns Hopkins University Press
701 West 40th Street
Baltimore, Maryland 21211

The Johns Hopkins Press Ltd., London

Library of Congress Catalog Card Number 75-3817
ISBN 0-8018-2654-3

For Monroe and Betty Spears
with deepest affection

Acknowledgments

The author and publisher gratefully acknowledge permission to reprint the following poems which originally appeared in the publications here noted: "Myth," sections 1 and 2, *Counter/Measures;* "Second Advice to the Poser," *Epoch;* "I Can Only Give You a Minute," "The Conclusion to the Renaissance," *Kansas Quarterly;* "The Verbal Emblem," *Literary Review;* "Snapshots," *Modern Poetry Studies;* "The Middle West," "Splicing," "The Musical Solution," "Daughter," *Pendulum;* "Song: The Edge," "The Touch," *Perspective;* "The Knowledge of Connaturality," *Prairie Schooner;* "Eye's Distance," "The Aristocrat," *Sewanee Review;* "with this ring I thee wed . . . ," "The Murder," *Shenandoah;* "Song: Hypochondria as the Basis for Conversion," "The Alter Ego," "Song of the Darkness," *Southern Review;* "Laurel and Hardy," *Southwest Review;* "The Story of Sam Bass: An Aria," *Strivers' Row;* "The Musical Emblem," *Virginia Quarterly Review.*

Contents

Foreword

To find a "first book" of poems, by a contemporary American, that I would compare to *The Heisenberg Variations*, I return to volumes like the *Ommateum* by A. R. Ammons, *Some Trees* by John Ashbery, Alvin Feinman's *Preambles*, James Wright's *The Green Wall*, and no more than two or three others. Bricuth is a fully formed poet, already battling for strength against a formidable triple composite precursor of Yeats, Stevens, and Hart Crane. Like his precursors he is a romantic expressionist, violently *within* the tradition, and his deepest affinities are with Crane and with Faulkner (whose early verse was also in Crane's shadow). As a southern poet, Bricuth recalls aspects of Poe (as Crane did), and like the midwesterner Crane, he has stylistic affinities with the fierce rhetoric of Tate and Warren. *The Heisenberg Variations*, despite the title's link with a theme of metaphysical indeterminacy, continuously dares an overdetermined and incantatory rhetoric, gaining thereby an immediacy of verbal power that goes back to the fountainheads of high romantic incantation, Shelley and Whitman. The risk, and sometimes the loss, for Bricuth is that he challenges comparisons all but impossible to sustain.

But the ambitions of this book, though enormous, give it an exuberance that has been absent from our poetry since Crane and Wheelwright, by which I mean a *formal exuberance*, very different indeed from the mock-vitalism of Ginsbergian bardism. Bricuth is a controlled if demonic artist, and like Shelley and Crane he tends to work within very difficult and demanding rhetorical and prosodic conventions, which he demonstrates to be anything but superseded. He is also, as any aspiring strong poet must be, an advanced critical consciousness, whose poems implicitly interpret, and so defensively seek to gain power over, the aspects of romantic tradition that he *must* dominate, if he is not to be crowded out into the living death of voicelessness. The double burden of continuously struggling for a formal innovation that yet does not break form, and also wrestling with the too-strong influence of the mighty dead, makes Bricuth's a very *difficult* poetry, as Crane's before him was startlingly difficult. Bricuth's best poems need endless rereadings and demand the exuberant study that an informed reader learns he or she must bring to visionary poetry, at its most intense and complex levels of meaning.

The strongest poems in this book, in my judgment, are "Song of the Darkness," "The Alter Ego," "Complementarity," the prose-poem "A New Model of the Universe," and all eight of the major poems in part 3, "From the Spirit of Music." But among these eight, I would single out as crucial and powerful texts "The Musical Emblem," "The Verbal Emblem," and, above all, "Circles"; for these three, and probably also "Song: The Musical Solution," are the work by Bricuth that marks him as an inevitable and central poet in American romantic tradition, and I believe that it is from these poems that his art must develop, if he is to impose himself fully on that tradition.

For want of space, I shall comment only upon "Circles," which joins the work of A. R. Ammons as our largest contemporary extension of Emerson's dangerous essay of the same title. Bricuth's "Circles," which ends this first circle, his book, begins as ironic autobiography, showing us the ephebe or beginning poet in his pugnacious origins, "Fighting to play at once all / The notes, fast and loud, / All the time," a perfectly knowing and accurate summary of the poetry he now writes, both in its strength and in its most damaging limitation. These opening, self-revelatory octaves might as well be entitled "The Death of Hart Crane," for Crane crowds Bricuth out of the poem from the thirteenth stanza on. Crane's suicidal Shelleyan "leap of faith" is both Bricuth's ideal and his nightmare, his own compulsive search for the dark, broken "inward tumbling tower" that shall be his own Word, and not just his precursor's. Like the Nietzschean antithetical poet (Yeats and Stevens are the great exemplars), Bricuth "writes to negate the will," but his poetic will then proceeds in part 2 of "Circles" to attempt an audacious revision or misprision of Crane's "For the Marriage of Faustus and Helen." In the last section of part 2, which I find miraculous in its evocation of this poet's innermost phantasmagoria, Bricuth takes a stance in relation to his own vision that is almost unbearably complex and yet also constitutes one of the clearest and most profound insights into poetic belatedness that our tradition affords. In making his reader, as well as himself, "see how it must / Be this way and no other," Bricuth accomplishes a transumption or metaleptic reversal that would have delighted Nietzsche. "Circles" shows us what Bricuth can and must become, another strong, *antithetical* poet, another major continuator of the greatest of Western poetic traditions. *The Heisenberg Variations* will be seen, someday, as the advent of a crucial voice and a central poetic career, worthy of its origins in Hart Crane and his fellow poets.

Harold Bloom

Yet the reinterpretation of the question of being as such tends to take the same form as the question of the essent as such, chiefly because the essential origin of the question of the existent as such and with it the essence of metaphysics remain obscure. And this draws all questions that are in any way concerned with being into the indeterminate.

In the present attempt at an "introduction to metaphysics" I shall keep this confused state of affairs in mind.

HEIDEGGER

I: Variables

Song: Hypochondria as the Basis for Conversion

Fallen on the time
When the pulse less steady
Starts the darkening mind
Musing on the body,
Every catch in the breath
Is the sickness unto death.

The back's real ache,
The eye's fictitious twitch,
The existential quake,
The sympathetic itch
Find their way to the head,
Bare the concept of dread.

What if minds crude
As sick-call in the service
Know no attitude
Between the dead and nervous,
Nor that body's made for
The spirit's stiff either/or?

True hypochondriacs,
Treading psychic nettles,
Sit on neural tacks,
Lie on moral needles,
Know body's ills are soul dissembling,
Fever and chills, fear and trembling.

Consciousness of self
Is that anguished gain

More valuable than health.
If imagined pain
Is what it takes to bring us to,
Then seize the dying point of view.

We're dying, doctor, dying
A fragment of a life,
And your sterile lying
And your clinic laugh
Cannot void the pen dipped
For the unscientific postscript.

Song: Eye's Distance

Kathleen views delighted
The far-off blink of dawn,
Notes with alarm
The closeness of the night,

Turns wide eyes wherever
Reflective eyes are found—
Always the edge
Encloses the brightened ground.

Limited as moonlight
Mirrored within a pool,
Puzzled, she stands
Aloof and looks at love.

The eye is a distant sense,
Makes the ordered bounds
Gross, human
Touch invades, confounds.

Each child's eyelid lowers
And only through too much
Love of what though
Touching does not touch.

Song: The Knowledge of Connaturality

Mere insinuation,
Lying at your side
I grasp sidereal drift,
The movement of the tide,
Each mute, physical attraction,
Reflex and chemical reaction.

If the soul is number,
Zero the center and
Love a long circumference
Collapsed as it expands,
Flesh points the way to live:
For knowledge gained, knowledge give.

Song of the Darkness

For Zelda Fitzgerald

Beneath a striped umbrella
Whose brown sunlight is rain,
My colors melt and run.
There's an old ache in my brain.

Set your face in a smile—
Rough grains within a glass
Will char the fragile neck.
The sick never get well.

What was the tune I laughed?
Just once I knew myself
Falls before the leaf
Broke the sun in half.

Darling, why don't you come?
We could waltz, and whirling, you
Would forget words they say,
Loving the steps I do.

Strands of the musical stave,
Twisted with spikes of time,
Score the white throat.
My wires catch and sting.

Who said it was ill
To love by giving pain?
If time cures the sick,
The sick never get well.

Song: The Edge

he takes the stairs from the third floor
of the hospital night a match's flare
a penitential rain is out
turning the collar of his coat
thinks—there no more

love is a passion death's another
what's behind when both are over
when love that knits the bodies' ache
and death annealing souls alike
are lost in one together

their love was no great passion but
this long death was passionate
as pain's ecstatic as hand would cover
hand drugs put her under
and heart is numb yet

he goes the wet street not caring
freedom like this is fearful foreign
out after something bitter now
believer in love finding how
sharp's the edge of sharing

Splicing

careful if you watch they
exit from the backseat
of the taxi the boss
con molto vivace
and the honey slow it
right there voila now the
appearance allegro
con brio in the corner
of the frame of what we'll
call la grande dame sans merci
holding as if she knew
what she were doing what
can only be a Magnum pop
a very good year for
shooting slow motion stop
as the first bullet tears
into his head thrown back
and to the side slowly
drifting toward the pavement
already dead bullet
two fired at this point where
the small puff and the violent
dislocation of the
okay cut now it's
honey's turn a peroxide
of fear look at that mouth
slow it right there run it
back that's a part of her
shoulder disintegrated
by bullet number three

look at her face she knows
this is it pow dead center
of the left maxillary
sinus spun left to right
legs tangled floating toward
the sidewalk scherzo speed
up uninjured injured
third party dances briskly
out of the frame no names
on them yet yes indeed
beautiful technique
always tell an artist
by economy of force

with this ring I thee wed and with this fist I punch your head

said, "because I only say this for your own good,"
said, "look, would I tell you this if I didn't love you?"
she began to get that look said "bastard you
bastard," said, "look, if we got married, with me
you get me, but with you, there's thisWHOLEdamngang"
if I stop I am dead "your mother's
crazy whose isn't that's a free one,
but your father   jesusgod   he's like a character
in Dickens who keeps getting drunk till his head flops in the stew,
and your brother who was knocked out of a tree with a rock
cars and football and baseball and cars
                                                    and he *wants* to *talk* to *me*?"
she breaks in here with "bastard you bastard" but *I* am ROLLING
"and your sister lays in wait looks like
something the cat had in the alley last night,
see, with me there's me but with you
there's this wheel barrel full of crazies, now,
if we got married" when the fan hits grabbing
her hands to keep from being killed this
is an historical explanation of the scar
on my forehead and that remark about women
referring everything to themselves hey goddammit
cut that out   that *hurt*

Villanelle: "We're dancing now . . ."

We're here with all our friends we've known since college.
Our teeth are straight and our hair is mostly blond.
We're dancing now and you're missing it and it's great.

I've been practicing in my room all afternoon.
I've been trying to get the knack but I don't know.
These are the steps but they don't fit the music.

All the girls we brought are incredibly relaxed.
We understate and our eyes are mostly blue.
We're dancing now and you're missing it and it's great.

If this is amusing, I don't get the joke.
If this is a trick, I fail to see the humor.
If these are the steps, why don't they fit the music?

There's a girl here we'd really like for you to meet.
Her teeth are straight and her hair is mostly blond.
She's dancing now and you're missing it and it's great.

It's always like this. Why is it always like this?
Listen, we'd like to see you, but it's getting late.
If these are the steps, why don't they fix the music?
We're dancing now and you're missing it and it's great.

Daughter

She has put her family off.
Her mother
carves Old Testament letters.
She lives now with a lover.   And if

I call from an outside phone,
the vogue
of distance whirls up words at once
blue bitter and vague.

Bored with unique confusion
she believes
in causes,   seeking the one
with the relevant fishes and loaves.

I sit in the booth   so mad
I laugh
at caring   and kick hell out of
the door before I leave.

Second Advice to the Poser

(self-portrait)

    stare in the I,

                wear

a double-breasted suit or
    suit with a vest, sport
a Euclidean look, seem
    apt with check-
    book or tooth but
        in fact
        in secret toe-
    dance the tightrope be
        -tween
        number and dream

The Middle West

When the wrath of God rode down our street
Casting to four winds bricks and plaster,
We had just, I recall, sat down to eat
With the brand new Baptist pastor,
Talking sin
As the roof fell in
An unexpected disaster.

Later, singing beneath the debris
Out in the topsy-turvy street,
We dragged ("Nearer My God to Thee")
Grandma Pickle by her sneakered feet
In a prone position
In a dazed condition
Clutching two Bibles and a parakeet.

Talking Big

For Harry and Claudia

We are sitting here at dinner talking big.
I am between the two dullest men in the world
Across from the fattest woman I ever met.
We are talking big. Someone has just remarked
That energy equals the speed of light squared.
We nod, feeling that that is "pretty nearly correct."
I remark that the square on the hypotenuse can more
Than equal the squares on the two sides. The squares
On the two sides object. The hypotenuse over the way
Is gobbling the grits. We are talking big. The door
Opens suddenly revealing a vista that stretches
To infinity. Parenthetically, someone remarks
That a body always displaces its own weight.
I note at the end of the gallery stands a man
In a bowler and a black coat with an apple where
His head should be, with his back to me, and it is me.
I clear my throat and re (parenthetically) mark
That a body always falls of its own weight.
"whoosh-whoom!" sighs the hypotenuse across,
And (godknows) she means it with all her heart.

The Conclusion to the Renaissance

For Bill Heyen

In the backyard bluejays
are strafing the neighbor's cat.
It is "Buster"—
fat, black, furry, the spoiled
pet of two old people,
a sybaritic walterpater cat that
catches some tint dying every moment,
would
wear carpet slippers and a red
velvet smoking jacket   but
momentarily
has foregone the general
savoring of experience
while a lumbering bluejay,
head
like a blunt door-knocker,
drops its Stuka flaps, braces
the tines of its feet, and
backing
air-oars
at the bottom of an arc, pounds
die welt als wille nicht vorstellung on
Buster's dream-wagon.

I Can Only Give You a Minute

Miss Brickhouse, take a letter. *Yes, sir.* Dear Sir: *Wait . . .*
All right, Dear Sir: In reply to your *Wait . . . All right.*
In reply to your ransom note *Wait . . . All right "Dear sir:"*
Am I going too fast? *No.* In reply to your ransom note
Wait. of the 17th instant *All right.* offering the safe return
Wait . . . All right . . . "to your ransom note" of the 17th instant
offering the safe return *Wait.* of my wife and children, *All right*
"offering the safe return" of my wife and children, *Wait.*
I wonder how you arrived *Wait . . . All right "of my wife and children,"*
at the figure you quote. *Wait . . . All right.* Please read that back.
"Dear Sir: In reply to your random note" ransom note *"ransom note*
of the 17th instant offering the safe return of my wife and children,
I wonder how you arrived at the figure you quote."
It strikes me *Wait.* that the price *All right.* of fifty thousand dollars
Wait. It strikes me that the price of fifty thousand dollars
All right. for five people *Wait . . . "dollars"* fifty thousand dollars
for five people *All right.* is completely out of line. *Wait . . . "for five people*
of fifty thousand dollars for five people is completely out of line. *All right.*
After all *Wait.* my wife *Wait . . . All right.* After all, my wife *Wait*
is over fifty years old. *All right . . . "my wife"* After all, my wife is over
fifty years old. *All right.* And my oldest son *All right.* I don't even like. *W*
"over fifty years old" And my oldest son I don't even like. *Wait.*
I don't even like. *All right.* Perhaps I might go as high *Wait.*
       as seventy-five hundred
All right "don't even like." for the two little girls *Wait . . . All right.* for th
two little girls *Wait.* as high as seventy-five hundred for the two little girls
All right. but that *Wait . . . All right.* is my top price. *Wait.*
Expecting to hear from you *Wait . . . All right.* in the very near future *Wa*
one way or the other, *All right.* I remain, *"my top price"*
Expecting to hear from you *All right.* in the very near future *Wait.*

one way or the other, I remain, *All right "in the very near future"*
       one way or the other
in the very near future, I remain, *Wait . . . All right.* Yours truly,
All right. Bernard J. *Wait "Yours truly,"* Yours truly, Bernard J. *All right.*
I remain, Yours truly, Bernard J. Pike *Wait.* truly, Bernard J. Pike *All right.*
Yours truly, Bernard J. Pike *Wait.* Bernard J. Pike *All right.* B. J. Pike

Abstract

chinese tallow tree in winter
laceofblackdots   like the ray
swung upsidedown at
the dense netted eye

scissoredbrainhazepulsingwarm
the crackle of electric wire
blue arcs   within the blur
boiling in the nerve storm

an upturned car smokes   wisps
curl around the wounded wheel
air is cold   earth is cold
the snow falls in a red swirl

ruptured vessels in the field
thread the blots of winter myth
the tallow tree   the wine sky
leak from the corners of his mouth

Bomb Collage

(The Poe School Bombing, Houston, 1959)

Dust splinters, spins, waves blunt
Breakback against blueangled roofs, the stunned
Windows of a scratched, sunlit block. Silence, coughed
Blood. Odors. The raw debris.
The zeroman whose suitcase coiled and clicked
Has wiped the schoolyard like a slate.

Inside his skull both hands burst
Into a frame, blossomedandbits fell
In hooks of light, shreds on bladed
Stems. A harsh, whirling light. Clay-
Crumbling grip in his, he scrapes from blue
The depth to be crushed out.

Trapped in the cubist wedge
Of dance or play,   aiming the disin-
tegrative spike within,   square
Receding square bent and slashed, the children
Blow the man apart,   bright chatter
Of light's sluiced ferocity.

"hecamefromthatdirection   no   threeorfour
witnessessaythatwashisson   about
seven   yes   that'sityes   thebombwasthere
no   thebiggestpieceispart
ofoneofhisfeet   notifyoudidn'tknow   i'vegotthemhosing
theroofsbothsidesstraightback"

Surreal and small like dolls
Nudged and pressed by the fist of ten sticks

Of dynamite, which formula for those
Whose edges whine as their bodies mix—
The unseen, slow-collapsing equa-
tion where light stops?

I cannot, no, nor do I mean to bring
Comfort to those bewildered parents ten years
In wait. We move in two dimensions.
Appearance is real. I speak of what appears.
These reconstructions make long chains of sound.
Man is a thing among other things.

The Murder

My friend's younger brother robbed and murdered,
His body two weeks rotting in a field,
Calls demanding ransom, the rasped
Voices that whisper perversion,
A death among ads
Without a private life or private grief,
The soiling pity of the press that blackens the hand,
The prying kindness of neighbors, old
Ferocious animal heart in its sweating closet,
The slide-bolt masturbation of personal fear,
And in the midst of it all
That large close-knit family turning,
Turning
Like a man fallen among wild dogs.

What shall I say? That there are good and bad,
Murderers and victims? Make the expected statement,
Humane against human, emotion checked by thought?
Say that I will justice, when I want revenge? Say
I stand so much above common men
No man's evil can infect me? Shall I lie,
Having looked in the vexed heart, and say
Were it the need that singly or in a group
I go to find the man who did this,
And going
Took the blue-blunt gun, slow knife,
The quiet voice
To turn and point and hurl the mob
That that man, once captured, that frightened man
Would live to plead his case,

Would live, a life appealed
Through comic trials, to pray
For life? Not beg in a scorched whisper?
Not scream and darken in a field?
                              Where is the charred prey
Of the wild dogs?

The Alter Ego

Turn (allegro)
On balconies or in the drifting car
His unplanned movements trigger quick reactions   where
Wave-like shadows shifted into place
Re-shift, rippling out across a sea of faces.
The national surrogate of speed in action,
He bears one shadow there whose movements are
A psychic counter-turn, the blocking figure
Spawned in the racial mind, the armored fervor
In the simple aim.

Counter-turn (adagio)
              I imagine grey eyes
That know the wind and wave and take their ease
Although the darting body is dorsal-finned
That hovers by—no catching at safety for
Those who swim the farthest from the shore,
Those who sail the closest to the wind—
The dark self that cannot be escaped
When life in the winding minute's telescoped.

Stand (allegro)
Praise Light for the framed instant's animation,
For any brusque wave or casual motion, each thriving sight and
Sound, each life-affirming gesture which a young man in his mood
May, with a vigorous will, diffuse about him,
Praise harder now the second brings the time that tests all praising
When, raising his hand, turning, laughing at something a friend
        has said,
His shadow an instant blocks the sun, the index finger tightens,
The shark-nosed bullet bites into his head.

Complementarity

Faith begins in dreams, guilt, the blurred
Flash of a raw meal, mornings, walking
The streets his mind like night, barely awake,
Abrupting the carved animals that bleed to faces,
Fuse to an old face, fear, a tongueless
Night-punishment, his land tricked and brought low, the brothers'
Unclean communion . . .

                              Defeated? Tell.
Who defeated *him*?   Betrayed.
These shadows' sudden folding along a wall, sheep
That made him tremble as a child, shadows
That are no shape, nameless, his dead brother.
Come close, they melt in crowds, become a crowd.
Spiralling to sleep, they wait at the edge . . .
The shadow . . . the edge . . . waiting . . .

                              And then he found them.
Crude as streets, in shops, in restaurants, jabbering,
Pushing in. He sketches in the cafes, bathing himself
In sound, the spittlewarm smear of thick accents,
Watching the dark, strong-scented women—tainted, loud.
He sits listening in a corner poised, wiping
The infected silver with his napkin, tensing
In a pent-up, hysterical ecstasy of fury.
This is the hidden animal that devoured the father.
He is the youngest child. He knows the one who loves,
Is known. He and the father are one.

                              Peddlers—
Simple, tragic? Sensual clowns? That moist,

Guilt-loving creed of pathos, the sunset-long
Female moan when the maimed animal
Breaks the glass edge of the lighted arc. No.
He is the loyal son.

                Wiping the blade of his knife,
He cuts the unsalted loaf, drinks the wine,
Tastes a hatred crushed from sounds in air,
Knowing the years to come and years to wait,
Slander, betrayal, the contemptible lie that he
Is one of these, let anyone say it, no, let *them*
Say it, they long to atone, are weighed, once
The knife is lifted, no voice can save them, he must wait,
It shall be consummated,
They long for him, wait,
Deep down they fuse in an old belief,
He and the father are one, the pure in heart
Hate one thing, he tenses, he strokes the blade of his knife.

II: The Voice While It Lasts

She had meant much to him, she had made him a poet, and thereby she had signed her own death warrant.

KIERKEGAARD

Song for Three Voices: You, Me, and Him

To make a voice frees him from the body. "Called:
　How to say the same about the Same."
　　Words on the page can counterfeit a voice.

He's late: making means he must destroy.
　"Who knows if a measured voice is sincere?"
　　Don't break down the rules, don't break up the game.

"This repetition's dull enough for words."
　The silence of the father speaks in the son.
　　Words on the page can counterfeit a voice.

Will wills the disillusion of the will.
　"What art does he know except revenge?"
　　Don't break down the rules, don't break up the game.

"We are the poem. The speaker himself is spoken."
　He aims to build a counterworld as if . . .
　　Words on the page can counterfeit a voice.

"That's called: How to say the Same about the same."
　Will wills the dissolution of the will.
　　Words on the page can counterfeit a voice.
　　Don't break down the rules, don't break up the game.

The Story of Sam Bass: An Aria

For Alicia

Well, what do you do when they call you Sam Bass? The hump-back man in the play says, They call me a villain, then I'll be one. And Sam Bass was an outlaw. He broke the laws of the great state of Texas, and when you break the law, they hunt you down and kill you. The Rangers hunted down Sam and shot him dead outside of Round Rock. That Rangers is an interesting word. They're out on the range and they range over it and so they're called Rangers. You see, one of the things I like to do is explain things and some of the things I explain best are words. Well, here I am named Sam Bass with a fearful precedent hanging over my head. Can I redeem the name? Will people say years from now, Oh you mean the good Sam Bass, why I thought you meant the outlaw. Or does the name sink me? Lord knows, all my best instincts are for lawbreaking. Ordered destruction is the phrase I like to use. I'm always making up phrases and when I quote somebody it's generally me. I do this because I have a lot of friends who wouldn't spend a dime on anything I said so when I want to say something I pretend I'm quoting someone famous and then they listen. I reckon that among my friends I've been the making of Shake-speare and Plato because just on account of my pretending to quote these two bozos and other pilgrims like them they all of a sudden picked up a name and a following and now when I say, Well, you folks recall what Plato or Shakespeare or one of those jaybirds said, and run off one of my phrases they fall all over each other trying to get the damned thing laminated so they can carry it in their wallets. Words to live by, I call it. Well, here I am named Sam Bass with a story to tell about a man named Sam Cass. You can see why I was going on about my name. When I first met Sam Cass I said to him, My name's

Sam Bass, and he said, My name's Sam Cass. I thought he was pulling my leg and you know back down in my part of the country there are pards that'll pull your leg and you'll walk with a limp for the rest of your life. So he says, My name is Sam Cass, and I thought he was puttin some fun on me. Well, I gave him a mean Texas look, a-package-of-Pell-Mells-and-a-red-sodawater red-neck look, and old Sam says, It's a strange coincidence ain't it. I mean about the name, he says. Now you've got to remember that Sam was from Boston and I naturally figured that he was tryin to smartmouth me. First of all, he said his words kinda funny and then he has this name that rhymes with mine but's not mine and he has a face sharp enough to chop wood and a little babypiddle moustache that got leaked across his upper lip. You see, Sam's father was rich as a Cretan and Sam was the cheapest man in the world so when it came to growing a moustache Sam didn't waste any hair. He grew just enough hair to give you the idea that what it was was a moustache and if you got that idea that was enough. I must say that Sam was the sparest meagrefeatured man I ever met. You know up in New England they have a phrase, Use it up, wear it out, make it do, or do without. I sometimes think that that was the way Sam treated himself and God knows he treated everybody else that way. That's a real phrase from New England just in case some of you got to thinking that that was something I made up. Well, this Sam Cass had a wife named Helen. He also had a dog named Rover but that forms no part of the story. Helen thy beauty is to me as those nice old barks of yore. And if you ever saw Helen you'd just bet that she could bark. She had a body like an axe-handle and she was one of those Libbers. I met a couple of em in a bar once and bought em some beer while we listened to Buck Owens. One of em had a real nice ass on her but the other one kept saying that she wanted me to treat her like a sister cept she looked like my brother. Well, you recall that when the Rangers strung up Sam Bass just outside of Round Top, old Sam looked around and said, I commence to see how this could be dull. And God knows that's the truth. And it just goes to prove what I said about Sam Cass, because Sam Cass was generous to a fault but he never took a bath. Now that's a paradox, and being a thoughtful person I naturally come down hard on paradox. You'd say, How can you be generous to a fault and the cheapest man in the world? Well, Sam had this all figured out. He'd come up to you and say, You can have anything I got, but then you saw that nothing he ever had was worth a damn. It was a phrase that Sam Cass would give you the shirt off his back, but that it smelled so bad nobody would take it. I just made that up right then. Now for years, I think eight but I could be wrong, time's got a way of slewing off from me some days, for years the main object of Sam's cheapness'd been Helen. They fought about everything but mostly about Sam's cheapness and when Helen was pressing Sam pretty hard and harrying him good and when it looked like Sam wasn't going to be able to do anything with words, why he'd just flick out a bony fist and clock Helen up the side of the head. I must admit that Helen had a way, with one side of her face all red and puffy, of rolling up her eyes and throwing back her head and howling, Goddammit, Sam Cass, you bastard, that was truly winning. Now this Helen was a funny girl. I recall once how she emptied a package of razor blades into Sam Cass's bath water. Sam Cass always used to say she was changeable. I remember once he said to me, You know, Sam, that Helen is a changeable woman, almighty changeable. Well, I reckon you already have the idea that this Sam Cass didn't have much of a way with words like me. He didn't understand them and that was bad for Helen because if he'd've understood them she wouldn't have got clocked on the head so often. I'd say that the number of people in this world who understand words as good as me you could count on the fingers of your left hand. Some people don't care about words and some think you got to court em but I've noticed that the people who always had the most out of me were the ones who treated me like dirt and I've always thought that was the way to get the most out of anything. I'm as common as my words and I treat em common. Now you see, that was just the problem with Sam Cass. He didn't have the common touch. And add to that, he was the boringest man alive. Yet sometimes he could do things truly comical. I remember once asking some of the boys, Does it seem that Sam Cass tends to dull on you after a space? Dull? Ouee! Sam Cass could bore you so bad it'd make a Quaker bite on a bullet. So after about eight years Sam's cheapness started to dull on Helen. Now you remember that when the Rangers hit Sam Bass on the head with a rock at Spindletop, the leader of the posse was a man named Jeff Hartman. He was a German fella and a romantical cuss and he asked old Sam if he had any last words to say before they poured kerosene all over him and set him on fire. You can see from that Jeff was also a little slow because who wouldn't have words to say if an owlhoot told you that as soon as you stopped talking they were going to warm their coffee pot on your ribs. I figure that one way or another that says a lot about life. There's lawbreakers like Sam Bass and there's

Rangers like Captain Jeff Hartman and it's all just one destruction after another. Because you remember that in the folksong Jeff Hartman is shot dead by a cowboy named Claude who had a rip in his jeans. You also recall that Claude was a half-breed but that never came out in the song. And it strikes me that there's another song in that fact alone. Well, Helen'd had about all she could take of Sam's cheapness and had commenced to make her displeasure unknown. Now say what you will about Sam, he wasn't stupid. He could read signs as good as any scout and knew their wherefor and he knew that either he was going to have to uncheap for a while or else he was going to have to clock Helen on the head a lot harder and a lot oftener and Helen's head had commenced for a while now to seem downright periphrastic. That periphrastic is an interesting word. It means using more words than you need to say something, kinda talkin in circles like. And you see, that was just Sam's problem. If he'd've used more words he wouldn't've had to hit her so often, but once he started to hit her the natural periphrastic took over and no doubt but he glossed the text more than was needed. Now bellied up to an increased work of glossing and the margin already near full up with marks, Sam saw that he was going to have to back off some. He'd noticed that of late Helen had commenced to talk to herself and that she just kept on talking. She'd also get a kinda funny look in her eyes and stare at her face in the mirror, sorta like she didn't recognize it anymore. So Sam decided to give her a surprise. It'd begun to come on to their eighth anniversary and me being Sam's best friend and just about the only person in the world that would talk to him, he invited me to go out with them for a big evening. Now you recall that when Sam Bass was laying there on the ground saying his last words with old Jeff Hartman standing over him with a kerosene can in his hand, everytime Sam would pause for a breath and break the natural rhythm of his discourse Jeff would raise the can kinda threatening like and old Sam would have to stop all of a sudden in midbreath and start talking again. Well, this had gone on for a while when Jeff Hartman started whistling a tune. The tune was called I'm Headin for the Last Round-up, and Jeff had a beautiful clear voice and pretty soon one of the Rangers pulled out a jug and started playing and first one and then another of the Rangers commenced to joining in and what with this and what with that before you know it all the Rangers (next on to twenty of them so the story goes) had gathered around old Sam who was still talking and were just singing fit to make you cry. Well, I think that goes to show where the real values are in life. Because before they roasted Sam and cut him up in pieces they asked him if there was any song he'd particularly like to hear and he said, Yes, would they sing The Red River Valley, and they didn't know the tune so Sam whistled a few bars and they picked it right up and then he asked them if they knew Campfires in the Valley and that recollected them of their original purpose and Sam had to start talking again something fierce. Now the best thing about Sam Cass was that no matter what he had to do he always did what he wanted to. I called it arbitrary. I said one day to some of the boys, You know, that Sam Cass has a way of putting his arbitrariness on things mad enough to make you spit. Of course, since I hadn't made as if I was quoting someone they didn't think of what I said worth a damn. Some people are like that and I think there's a great lesson to be learned from it but since that lesson has nothing to do with the business at hand I just leave it out as a hint because as I reckon you've figured out besides being smart myself I'm also the cause of smartness in others. I just made that up right then and as I read back on it it strikes me as pretty damn good. Well, this Sam Cass takes us out to dinner at a hamburger stand and says, It's on me, eat as much as you want. Next on to the fourth hamburger and the sixth beer I was starting to get a little puffed, but Helen was in homely heaven because Sam had done all this just for her and he was going to take us to a drive-in movie afterwards and then we were going to end up the evening at a beer joint outside of town. And all evening Sam had been dropping hints that he had Helen an anniversary present and as he hadn't ever given Helen anything but hard times I was curious to see the look on Helen's face when she opened the package and the boxing glove jumped out and hit her on the nose. Because I knew that's just what it was. You might say I knew that because I knew Sam Cass's sense of humor and that there wasn't nothing he enjoyed more than a good joke and I hadn't ever seen Sam Cass put as much effort into anything like this evening that somebody didn't end up getting crap in their eye and as I knew it wasn't going to be me, because if it was, Sam Cass was going to get his head kicked up his ass, then it had to be Helen. Now you'd say, How come a gentleman like me stands around all evening while Sam Cass puts the mean fun on Helen? Well, now it strikes me that somebody that'd marry Sam Cass in the first place put the mean fun on themself and in the second place I'd encompassed a lot a beer and in the third place Helen was Sam's wife and I didn't have no sayso in the matter and in the last place being a gentleman of the old school I don't generally fight over an ugly woman. This Helen was no ideal beauty though there was certain lines near her eyes that gave out to indicate how she might have been tolerable to look at once before she fell in with wordless Sam and he got to glossing her text. Old Sam was smart as the dickens and I expected some fun that was truly inventive out of the evening. That dickens is an interesting word. It's an old time phrase for the devil and there sure as hell was something bedeviled about Sam at times. Sam was a tinkerer and Helen figured as how he'd tinkered up something for her with his own hands and I'd figured as how he had too and that Helen was going to unwish that figure before the evening was over. Well, you recall that when the Rangers stuck Sam Bass with a knife at Red Rock there was a coot name of Nick along who was trying to get the reward on Sam's head and you also recall the incidents that occurred as they're recorded in the folksong and what that singing caused in West Texas with the events at Uvalde and Hellgate and the other song that arose out of that. So as Sam Bass was laying there with his life pumping out through the bullet hole in his chest they said, Sam, do you have any last words? And old Sam looked up and said, Well, it certainly seems like I ought to as whatever I say now is likely to become current and gain a name and a following. Now of course, I've had a name and a following for years, says Sam, but the name got too well-known and the following finally caught up to me. And I reckon as how that says a lot about life because you recall that when I held up the stage between Last Chance and Kneadsville there was a book drummer on board with a cast in his eye that was mad as the devil. But when I shot him right through the third button on his vest he calmed down all of a sudden. So I guess now I'm going to have to pay the price for my wilful arbitrary ways. Well, I recollect as how I illustrated that Sam Cass had a way of doing what he wanted no matter what the conditions were and I figured that that was sure enough what was going to sneak up and clock Helen on the head because when we were sitting in the beer joint after a few rounds and Sam took this package out of his coat and set it on the table in front of Helen I didn't know whether to duck under the table when she opened it or stay around and take my chances for the fun. Now just as you can't tell a book by its cover, sometimes you can tell a gift by its box. The box was wrapped fancy and that immediately made me suspicion something. It was about an inch high, an inch and a half wide, and six inches long or just about the size of a box for a wrist watch though if I'd've heard it a tickin I'd've gone under that table so fast I wouldn't've had time to say good-bye. Now as Helen sat there lookin at the box I got ready to say a memorable phrase for the occasion. If it was a watch I was going to say, Well, Helen, better a clock on the wrist than a clock on the head anyday, huh? But I would've bet my life that it wasn't a watch because you see as I said earlier I knew Sam Cass's sense of humor and that old Sam would sit there whistlin a tune and calculatin and integratin and differentiatin as to how we thought it was a watch from the size of the box and as to how that was just what he wanted us to think because that misthought was to be the basis of the fun. But then I thought maybe he'd ring the changes on us by figurin that if we knew his orneriness and how he'd belie the box, why then he'd just belie it once more by really puttin a watch in there. At any rate I got ready to say my phrase if it was a watch or to hurry up think of another phrase if it wasn't and Helen was takin off the wrappin real tender like because Sam had wrapped it up with his own hands and I was sittin there thinkin,

Helen, you poor old sonuvabitch, he's done you again. Well, she got it unwrapped and she set the box in front of her and she looked over at Sam kinda lovin and she put her hand on his and said, Sam Cass, this is the happiest night of my life. And Sam in his sorta off-hand sidewinder way says, Hon, I purposed it to be a night you'd never forget for the rest of your life. Well, I bit my tongue good and hard over that one but Helen was so wrapped up she didn't notice and so she kisses her lips at Sam and she turns back to the box and slow and tender she lifts the lid and there sits a brand-new shiny harmonica. Well, I reckon as how if Sam had picked up a beer bottle and clocked Helen eight or ten times running on the head he couldn't have produced a look of downright stupefaction to match the one on her face because after a minute she pointed a long finger at the box and said kinda unbelievin like, It's a goddam harmonica, and old Sam leans over and says kinda casual, Yeah, I always did wanta learn to play one of them things. Well, I couldn't hold it in no longer and mayhap some of you are wonderin how I held it in this long but I commenced to laughin like I ain't never laughed in my life and Helen commenced to sobbin and Sam reached over and picked up the harmonica and started pickin out a tune. By now I was laughin so hard that the rhythm of my laughin had got in with the rhythm of my breathin and my heart beatin so that I was fit to expire and I couldn't say hardly a word and Helen was just a sobbin and a sobbin and every so often she'd vary the melody that Sam Cass was pickin out with a gasped phrase such as You cheap-shit two-bit sonuvabitch or Sam Cass, you raggedy-assed bastard or some other like words. And Sam stops playin for a moment and says kinda drawlin out of the side of his mouth, It ain't cheapness, it's economy of force, and that's the first law of nature, and then he commences to play again and I started laughin so hard I banged my head against the side of the booth. Well, there I was laughin in rhythm and Helen sobbin in rhythm and Sam Cass playin the melody and though it only lasted a couple of minutes it seemed like forever. All kinda goin around in circles like from the beer. I finally straightened myself out enough to speak a phrase and I turned to Helen and said, Now lookit here, Helen, there ain't so much difference between a watch and a harmonica, why old Plato said it hisself, he said, I'd rather have a harmonica than a watch any day of the week because with one of em time runs you but with the t'other you run time. And right about here old Sam makes a fancy run on the harmonica and Helen starts sobbin again fit to beat the band and a course I wasn't able to hold back no longer and I commenced to laughin again like judgment day. So you recall that when Sam Bass was a dyin and the Rangers asked him if he had any last words he looked up at Captain Jeff Hartman and says, Jeff, I'd like to hear one more song, and Jeff looks at his old turnip and says, It's gettin kinda late, Sam, I don't know if we have time, and Sam says, Take the word of a dyin man, Jeff, 'cause dyin men alwayst tell the truth and generally say somethin important too that never fails but to gain a name and a followin, there's always time for another song. And it strikes me as how when you think on it there's a whole nother story in them words alone.

A New Model of the Universe

The best image to sum up the unconscious is
Baltimore in the early morning. JACQUES LACAN

Here is an equation that I have been working on my blackboard
for years:

$$3b + \text{the moon} + 5 \text{ seconds} = \text{what?}$$

Like most people you will say that $3b$, the moon, and 5 seconds
can't be added because they are not things of the same order.
To which I reply—"That's obvious." Anyone could add up $1 +
2 + 3 + 4$ and get 12. Where's the glory, where's the self-
overcoming in that? as Nietzsche used to shout. Besides it is a
practice designed to arrest thought and suspend inquiry; it is
self-negating: when things are equal, they vanish. And here, of
course, is the beauty of my equation—that difficult equation that
I have been working for years on my blackboard—it is clearly
impossible. No doubt, you will point out that the real difficulty
of this impossible equation is not in the terms $3b$, the moon, and
5 seconds but in the signs $+$ and $=$, which obviously make de-
mands that the terms can't meet and that anyone who makes
demands is being difficult, if not impossible, and should be put
out. All of which is true though it must be rejected in the name
of logic. For suppose we substituted for the signs $+$ and $=$
the picture of an apple and the stopper from my hot water
bottle, why then the whole thing would acquire an unfamiliar
look that strikes at the very basis of the principles of identity and
non-contradiction and that series of natural numbers whose gen-
erative order proceeds n, $n + 1$, etc.

Some years ago I came very close to the solution of my
equation. In a morning of intense work followed by cramps
and a headache I rewrote the equation as

$$3b + (\text{the moon})^2 + 5 \text{ seconds} = \text{what?}$$

It was published in a journal whose name you would instantly recognize and excited immense interest until it was proved absolutely and completely false. I was disappointed as you can imagine. To be so near, and yet so far so good. However, at that point I made the observation that life is nothing but an endless rewriting of impossible equations experienced as the difficult, and I went back to work. But first I published that observation in a journal and it excited great attention. I got a letter from a man in Minneapolis who said he had the same name as mine except that he spelled it different.

I erased ten years' work from the blackboard and started over. You know how that relaxes you. I realized that the solution must lie in the concept of transposition. Something had to be taken from one side of the equation and transposed to the other side. I rewrote the equation as follows:

$$3b + \text{the moon} = \text{what?} + 5 \text{ seconds}$$

Now it was clear. On one side of the equation I had $3b$ and the moon and on the other side I had what? and 5 seconds—two things on one side and two on the other. Absolutely right. No, that's not right at all. I was just saying that to test you. Why you're even dumber than I am. Why am I wasting my time with this? Observe. If we add $3b$ and the moon, we get four things, whereas if we add what? and 5 seconds, we get six things, which is to say that $4 = 6$, and that can't be right. Now you will say, quoting Wittgenstein, that a number is the exponent of an operation and that while I am spending all my time looking down here at the big numbers in a row I should be looking up above and to the right for one of those little numbers and then I'd see something. That is a line of argument which I totally reject because I've never read Wittgenstein and I don't know whether you're quoting him correctly or not. Besides if I *had* read Wittgenstein you'd think that I was being influenced by him even in my determination not to be influenced by him which in a man of parts is intolerable. And if you ask who *have* been the great influences on my work I would say Freud, Wittgenstein, uh . . . What's-his-name Heidegger—*Martin* Heidegger—and Gracie Allen. Transposition. The secret is transposition. Or maybe transference. At any rate I was much closer to a solution with $3b$ and the moon on one side and what? and 5 seconds on the other than I was the way I first said it. So I'm sticking with that. Now you will ask, what about negative numbers, fractions, and transfinite numbers? Well, what about them? I realize that science is the process of endless questioning but you're getting to be a real pain in the ass.

Now let me see. What if I added two things to the left side or subtracted two things from the right side? You will say that that violates the rule that anything you do to one side of an equation you must do to the other side as well and why don't you go chase yourself too because I thought I almost had it. But wait. The problem with the equation is not the $3b$ or the moon or the what? or the 5 seconds or the $+$ or the $=$, it's all these damn rules that say if you do this then you have to do that. For after all, as Frege points out, number is objective and nonspatial just as Zuckerkandl says that music is objective and nonspatial and what the hell does that mean? No, the secret is transposition. It is by persistence in an intuition that all scientists have made their most important discoveries whether they were right or not.

So it is transposition, is it? Yes. The problem as I see it is one of analysis. After all, how can we add 3*b* and the moon and 5 seconds when we don't even know what they are? Take 3*b* for example. Is it 3 times *b*, or is it three *b*'s, or is it the figure 3 placed beside the letter *b*? All of these are different and each entails a different method. Or take the moon. Is it that bright thing we see in the sky sometimes, or is it two sounds, or is it three letters and a space and four letters—and is there a space at the beginning and a space at the end which of course will bring us dangerously close to the question of whether the series of natural numbers begins with 0 or 1 and whether 0 oscillates beneath each whole number. Or consider the term what? Is it four letters and a conventional gesture? Or is it rather the self-questioning concept of entity? Suppose we were to substitute for a self-questioning concept of entity a self-consuming artifact or a self-flushing toilet, the significance, as you can well imagine, would be entirely different which is to say wholly other. You will reply in your clever, relentless, and ultimately destructive way that by introducing a self-questioning concept I am preparing a logical trap-door through which I can drop at the first sign of trouble by claiming that the solution to the problem is a dissolution of the question which is simply to apply the argument of infinite regression or infinite divisibility so familiar from the paradoxes of Zeno though of course those same paradoxes are based on the logical flaw of treating space as infinitely divisible while refusing to do the same with time. To which I can only reply that you can't have a sign without analysis in the same way I can never have an onion without an alka-seltzer. That is a law of inference or interference, I forget which, and as such has the compelling quality of a given. And suppose that I *am* applying the argument of infinite regression and the Zenonian paradoxes so I lose my license and you can kick me in the head, right? Wrong. I'm still a human being whatever I say. For as Wittgenstein observes, "4.1212 What *can* be shown, *cannot* be said." More than a clever remark but less than a primitive idea.

4.1213   The solution lies in transposition.

4.12131   Now suppose we were to rewrite the equation as

4.12132 + 3b + the moon = what? + 5 seconds + 4.12133.

We'd be caught between the rock and the hard place, Bertie.

4.1214   Naw, we can't do that. You notice I say "we" because I am absolutely making you an accomplice in this garbage in case it flops and I need a dummy to hold the sack.

4.12141   However, if this analysis works out, I'll give you a footnote.

As Heidegger says, the only question is how does it stand with Being, which has been naively interpreted to mean how does it stand with the =, as if equality were identity were being, hoo-hah. Come right down here to this part of the blackboard that's still empty because we are going to rewrite this equation using a simultaneous transposition, an Orange Crush, and an old record of Irving Fazola playing "Spain" as

3b + what? = the moon + 5 seconds

which as an example of a simultaneous transposition is pretty sweet though we have come no closer to the nature of number, the convention of unitary wholeness, and the concept of entity than when we started. To which I can only reply that we've been driving for a while and we're no farther away and that if one is going to be held to this kind of accountability then I think it's just a shame because as Wittgenstein says logical propositions are never right or wrong, they either make sense or they don't. No doubt, you will point out that Quine has remarked of Frege's concept of number as classes of classes that here explication is elimination. However, since Quine is now out in paperback I really don't think that I have to take him into account because this is a serious discussion and not a chat in a bus station and I wish to God you knew what it meant to be an intellectual in times like these, too.

Surely at this point you will suggest that the real problem with my equation is not numbers but rather that it combines two opposing modes of thought—metaphor and metonymy, a synchronic equivalency and a diachronic analysis of a whole into parts. To which I can only reply that it is very dangerous to be smarter than the person who is doing the writing because you are likely to get your toe smashed in a footnote.[1] And let me add while we are on the subject that your reasoning shows why you are a reader and I am a writer, why you are sitting out there in a tract house in Omaha while I am sitting here in a tall building in Wilmington. Observe. If we rewrite the equation as

$$\text{what?} = 5 \text{ seconds} + \text{the moon} + 3b$$

then suddenly there flashes upon us a sense of recognition like when you see your face in the mirror after you've been drinking heavily. It has a certain uncanny familiar quality of unfamiliarity, a certain repetition-in-difference, its very otherness reconstitutes it as the same. In that instant, in that intuitive leap one realizes that if things weren't all equal there would be no question of inequality and vice versa, that what we are dealing with is a linked series of mutually constitutive oppositions like left and right, high and low, back and forth, smith and dale, and fric and frac. In a burst of white light it becomes clear that my equation is not an expression, or a proposition, or a statement—it is an embodiment. Like Walt Whitman or a great work of art or a fart in a crowded room, it doesn't have to argue, it convinces by its mere presence. To say that I can't add $3b$ and the moon and 5 seconds and make them equal what? is to misunderstand the arbitrariness that constitutes *dasein*, that peculiarly human arbitrariness that stands as the intermediate stage in the transformation of the random into the necessary as it selects from the random elements of the world an abbreviated set to arrange in an order whose meaning is conventionally understood to be meaningless because arbitrary but which forms the basis from which the elements of a conventionally necessary order can be constructed while at the same time that arbitrary meaningless order acts as a bulwark defending man against being overwhelmed by the infinite possibilities and combinations of the random because by now you have been looking for footnote 1 for a while and haven't been able to find it since it doesn't exist on the grounds that the threat is stronger than the execution and thus do I confute Wittgenstein and that stuff about numbers being opponents. You will say that putting in a footnote number and then not having a footnote is the violation of a convention but I was once in New York during a convention of the American Legion and frankly I don't see your reasoning because if a Cootie dropped a balloon full of water on your head from a seventh floor window what would be your reply to that, huh? No, I think that if you examine our rewriting of the equation once again you will be struck as I was by how much it reminds me of Emerson's remark that man's "victorious thought comes up with and reduces

all things, until the world becomes at last only a realized will,—
the double of the man." That is a remark of Emerson's that has
never been properly appreciated because Emerson never said it,
and in fact isn't that the way of the world? for my equation
is at once a reduction and a mirroring, it simultaneously occupies
a border point and is self-generative. As one is always, in such
situations, either a priori, a posteriori, a fortiori, or a capella
and as I have always chosen the latter realizing that it is the
voice that is the great equalizer because the great pulverizer in
its sovereign impulse to ride down all inequalities acknowledging
the likeness of sounds as the only true likeness at once self created
and self creating, so there is not and never was a solution to my
equation except the one it sang and, singing, made, in just the
same way that there never was a key to my garage door, for my
equation which makes unequal things equal is meant to stand
between me and the world, it is meant to domesticate the
violence of that world at the same moment that it exhausts my
desire for revenge on that world. It is magical. But of course
you will say So what? to which the only reply that I ever heard
that was any good and that I have always remembered in case
I ever got the chance to floor anybody with it was So anything!
And besides, haven't I just stolen fifteen minutes of your life that
you'll never get back and aren't you that much closer to death
in the sound of my voice? And *you* thought I was kidding. As
I look at my rewriting of the equation

what? $= 5$ seconds $+$ the moon $+ 3b$

I am moved to echo the words of that New England transcen-
dentalist whose name I can never remember when she said "I
accept the universe" as reflected in this new model.

III: From the Spirit of Music

All possible efforts, stirrings, and manifestations of the will . . . can be expressed by the infinite number of possible melodies, but always in the universality of mere form without the material, always only according to the in-itself, not to the phenomenon, as it were the innermost soul of the phenomenon without the body.

SCHOPENHAUER

This, indeed this alone, is what *revenge* is: the will's ill will against time and its "it was."

NIETZSCHE

The Musical Emblem

For Dr. and Mrs. W. R. McKee

I

Count the clock-face eyes of children housed
In dark, perdurable hospitals of the night,
The young men lost by fine miscalculations,
Some thousand brown men swirled and sunk
In the cracking of a fault, or half a million Asians
Wrapped in fire who, looking all alike,
Must count as one because the faces that the fire
Has kissed must look alike; arrange the vacant
Sun-shattering aircraft disintegrations,
Great railway wrecks in Italy or France,
Cars flipped and crushed or telescoped into eternal stations,
All crashes, the sure family in the tentative car
Singing down the highway on vacation,
Singing to the music of an instrument,
The harmonica or perhaps a guitar, an hour and we
Pass where steel scavengers ring in
Their centaur-wreck; measure the pestilence
And disease billowing like mist across
The will's sub-continent, apocalyptic figures,
Red, yellow, black, white, measure the casual
And the planned starvations, the hollow eyes
Spearing out of darkness, the running silica
Eyes of infants, the slivered metronomic
Arm within the flowing, air-blown sleeve
That clicks entropic arbitrary tunes
Whose harmony is forced in a closed system:
Least energy expended on one life
Disorders past all hope the hidden lives,
Pure time measured by the purely random
Stops short in gravity's contrapuntal strain.

An image of earth and fire and earth again
Forms in my mind. Mirror, or hour-glass, or both?
The disintegrating asymmetric hand
Beating on time's crystal windowpane,
The quartz clocks of embryo eyes run down,
Dying, all dying, four-figured, all myth,
Imagine the bullet dodged, the car swerved,
The plane missed that pours death on another head
". . . our faces, Lord, are hidden in pyramids of fire,"
But if the eyes are dead, undone the nerve's skein,
Dead and undone,
Who knows between the candle and the coin?
". . . hearing the pulse unravel at her wrist"—
Such breaking only can come back again
In broken images, if anything
Comes back then from that bewildering
Gratuity of death. I know no creature made of earth
But makes some shrill peep when it dies,
And does it, dying thus, leap up like flame
And from that death arise
And rising build the spiraling ground melody of grace
Braided with strains of pentacostal fire,
All fire and shadows whirled and turned as wind-whipped flame,
As flame before the livid, night-edged blast,
A music of cracked voices in the fire? That?
Or just some whirring canticle of waste and wrong?
Yes or no? I have listened these quick years
And for this death have never heard that song.

II

Such talk of earth and fire has force for minds
Grounded to an Eastern persuasion; minds like ours,
Now linear, now melodic, cannot catch
That elemental meaning nor understand
A form that's not conceptual incantation—
The mass of the dead and their expanded moment.
Singing down the half-light line of highway
One warm evening, the road unrolling before
Rolling up behind, singing a melody
Moving along a line, translating
Future into past, continuous as a violin's note
Woven on a violin string, relating
One non-existence to another, I was passed, passed,
And passed by cyclists coming from the dark,
Hurrying on, headlong, unknowing,
One rode the stuttering catapult to darkness
That at the sudden cross impacting, bled.
His shoulders limp with cervical despair,
I passed him on the road, gnarled and drowning in
The ocean of his blood.
                              Lapping his feet,
The gentle waves beat the pink outrigger's prow
Beneath the red and white umbrella's shade.
His eyes hardened to glass or glittering sand,
A foreign man ventricularly laid
Across the frangible line of land and sea
By breaking of the lesser ebb and flow
Was dying among men ignorant of his tongue,
Unable to speak of what he saw, yet
Some mystic says somewhere to see

We must have eyes incapable of tears.
I say that rhetoric is wisdom and the four
True virtues courage, insight, sympathy,
Lastly solitude, I claim that courage is
The form of these, and more, that rhetoric's
Our stance or our song, having experienced
The sense of waste and wrong. Our faults are fear,
Guilt, a need to love, the need
Of love. I purpose that nothing shall be lost
Or missed, nothing too brutal, coarse, hurtful,
Hopeless, silly, or full of the moment's frenzy
That courage can arrest in the movement of a song.
I praise a courage that is and needs no reason,
Wondering if it is such to trust what has been said
Should it appear I must be one of the kind
Who linger a distraught moment and pass
Like mist on the sun or wind across the grass
And do not leave a melody on the mind.

III

Considering this question or questions of this sort,
Aware how much of this is luck,
The complex variable, in the last resort
Made up of what we miss and what we lack,
Because even with the best precautions taken
Against the hundred adversaries I could beat,
Common sense is mistaken; it is a token;
It cannot stay the madman in the street.

I know that just outside the circle slumbers
In darkness something nameless and chaotic
Breeding a terror real *because* neurotic,
Kin to the Greek fear of irrational numbers.
Such apprehension proves proportion seldom
Lasts against the cause's chance effect.
Relation is incommensurable or random.
The reasoned life is a fragile artifact.

Great Christians and great hedonists agree
Upon a rule of life, living each day
As if it were their last. Who can foresee
The time, who can predict the way
That will dissolve a tenuous unity?
Live in the moment, the most that they can say.
But if two such extremes collapse in this,
How worry what we lack or what we miss?

So poems go a journey, but a few,
If the poet's heart is driven to despair,
Are curved back to that bleak point where
They first began. No, I am not one who,
Though preoccupied with death like many
Young people nowadays, can yet command
The elusive circle's grace or believe in any
Esthetic mode of life the young commend.

What road is left me? Or what have I left myself?
Once on a beach, once in the blinding street,
A man died before my eyes. No line is straight
But will in time turn back upon itself,

One late opinion holds. Desire misleads us;
Here art and science are equally a fraud.
Two moments death has touched my sleeve and thus
Of the jarring third moment I am afraid.

Religion has the future, art the past,
All that's real the ablative edge between.
I defy the word "real." What does it mean?
High art's simple question "Will it last?"
Faith encrypting what we hope is so?
Declensions of the moment; we choose the other.
All I know proves what I do not know. I know
We cannot have both, I suspect we cannot have either.

The legendary cyclists are dead, and all
Lines end in bold parameters of song.
The spinning weight of the sun cannot singe
The heart's blind eye or cure the mind's ill,
The end is there's no end, to keep or quit
A craft selected to make the moment mean,
If only in its turning. The craft is mine,
And mine to turn the phrase that curves the hurt.

I do the necessary work that must
By each one be redone who makes the eye
And tongue impress a tone or tint whereby
We salvage what we lack or what we missed.
I bind all inextricably and full
Of a self-made, self-amusing melody,
Between the doubled silences' slow fall,
Write to make the sound of what I see.

IV

Counterpoint

I make a song simple as the sun
To hold a thought circular and still,
I stare the apple spheres into one
And find the rim dying on the hill.

> How many have I known
> And taught the rule of melody,
> So that I have grown
> Tired of the cello's sound,
> Tired of the violin's tone?

Pooling dark rings of water under skies,
Sounding the long circumference they join,
I burn away the mist from dead eyes
That call two the candle and the coin.

> There have been a hundred
> String's subtle art has brought to me,
> Lately I have wondered—
> Where is the magic ground,
> Lost or fled or sundered?

I toss the pulsing apples in the air
To lay the brown horizon on a desk,
Turning the coin against the candle's flare,
Return the partial fire-dreaming disc.

> With too much explaining
> It has all seemed trickery,
> String's hard dramatic straining,
> Wherein the joy was bound,
> Was wavering, was waning.

The Aristocrat

Buster with his pork-pie hat above
That stone face, no fist, cop's foot, not curled
Lip, no eyes like angry marbles could
Dislodge or nudge the stiff agreement of
That fragile pair, possessed of authority because,
Silent within, at once self-amusing
And self-amused, he kept the personal style
That keeps through common nonsense an iron grace.

In vaudeville with a knockabout act he bent
Body to will, objects into props,
Renewing the aristocratic tradition of
Anything for the laugh. We are a mob in darkness,
Roaring our dangerous approval at the one
Who fights us, grave of face, to keep his hat.

The Touch

For Mona Van Duyn

Having attended her first piano requital in which
Numerous old musical scores were settled,
Chopin run over and rolled into a ditch
When Bach's light velocipede hard-pedalled
Went wheeling by, its (grand piano-) forte speed,
I blink at the chromatic scale of humane endurance,
Tone-, stone-, or simply deaf and dull
And wink in the first Euterpean lull
At the girl fit to ride down every nuance.

Only a small matter of a small only daughter,
Save music, as a kind of Vinteuil's phrase expanded
Of the heart-divining rhythm that can't be trained,
By absence must leave her seldom keyed to the laughter
Nor quite secure though beautiful, high-handed,
As one to whom things must often be explained.

The Verbal Emblem

For David Minter

It seems to me that I have found what I wanted.
When I try to put all into a phrase I say, 'Man
can embody truth but he cannot know it.' I must
embody it in the completion of my life.

YEATS, *January 1939*

I

Arthur Rimbaud and Laura Riding both
Renounced the craft or game of verse because,
Since poets choose the emblematic cause,
Words had turned to ashes in the mouth.
Trader of currants and dates, Rimbaud fled south,
Ran guns to Ethiopia, explored (Pater says
The artist runs a secret errand), and ran
Ten years a trading post, a diseased man,
Returned to die of cancer at Marseille,
His action imprecation, the wordless oath.

Laura Reichenthal alias Laura Riding
Married Schuyler Jackson and gave up
The ostensive writing out of verse to go
South to a Florida citrus farm growing
Grapefruit and oranges, but, unable to stop,
Even in self-imposed, symbolic hiding,
Interest in the verbal fruit and chaff trade,
She turned to dictionary work, each word
To have a single meaning, each meaning tried
For power to hold the truth, the word discarded
If found to be intractable or double.
With meanings and words, which is fruit, which chaff?
Perhaps the common mouth,
Denied the poet's ablative craft,
Does not savor the mixed taste of truth?

II

Yes, I sound superior to this, yet
Guess the time, still young but tired of drawing
Contrived conclusions from more contrived exempla,
Tired of slipping through a deft circumlocution,
Or perhaps, tired of turning the complex to the simple,
I quit the work of forging links of sound,
Word, idea, action, arbitrary
At best, to seek "objectivity and truth,"
Grown weary of my own will, surrendering
To an eventual will, or, faulting the medium of breath,
Cease shaking the chains by which the tongue is bound.
Weariness or timidity or what
Makes us quit the roles demanding much
And promising nothing makes me write to stop
By the exorcism of words what I fear most.

I aim to be as eloquent in my distress
And doubt as others writing from the ground of a belief
So solid they make their theme a defiant trust
Of all that affronts reason, belief being all.
Out of words doubtful for others I make
A personal speech—formal, old-fashioned,
Artificial, full of tricks. Indeed,
It is possible to be too subtle for too long
In making a style of gyroscopic poise,
Forgetting the crafted meaning's a mouthed noise
And the deepest wisdom only a whistled song,
But our naturalness now must be in all
Complexity. The world is only material
For song with those caught in the glittering net

That understands the surfaces of things,
And make the word become what it's about.
Soon the law of numbers will enforce
A sense of oneness beyond the lines of those
Who work equations of world and word. I think
There is no grove or garden we can get to
Where the act of naming's still fresh or fruit
Untouched by confusion of taste. We cannot redefine
Our words, we cannot run away, so
The meaning of this poem's neither what
It says nor what you know but some mixed thing
Made by tongue's abrading both. I sing

"Language is melodious commotion
That the few who move against its pure flowing
Are elided in the music of its going.
The most precise composers of emotion
Lose themselves within the aimless action
As the last form of meaningful distraction."

III

These lines are full of certain verbal tricks
Learned from the craftiness of Crane and Yeats
Whose different styles in our time have been,
Because some lives are symbols of an era, emblems
Of an old man's rage, of the desperation of young men.
Yeats, his rhetoric turned wisdom, all gesture and stance,
Dancing in ecstasy or rage, agèd,
Wrote words that seemed to dance upon the page,

Figuring the world a courtly, gyring dance, so
Reduced it to an arbitrary order,
Turned it to a song. Hart Crane believed—
Who knows what—maybe that love's the mode
Of knowledge, or that man's mind is God, or one
Of several hallucinations that spring
From writing of love yet never finding one
To love. In that precarious mixture of
Extravagance and precision, of lavish waste with
Residual brilliance, I see him standing, sick
On a ship's deck, beaten half senseless the night before,
The last years seeming a litany of sad mornings,
The future like a fleshless mouth, weary,
The husk of his life worn from his book, walk
To the stern in ashen sunlight, fold his coat,
Climbing the rail, balance alone words
That can be said in praise of any moment,
Rhetorical as ever, fall silent to the sea.

I have made a poem out of poets' lives
In that extended process of naming that,
When all's said, is all our art. I admit
I deal in a large manner with those that are
Better poets than I, but consider,
I name all with honor here, affection,
Whether their acts were words, or words action.

Laurel and Hardy

For Larry and Faith

I

wide tie, wing collars, vest, and derby hats—
                                    "don't
you kick *me* in the shin"—that spiff
boiled front of salad days—"you . . .
keep your distance"—the thin and the fat
ruined gentleman aiming a delirious
Ford with a broken knee, huffing
an upright piano
ten flights up,
fishing off a dock—"tell me,
why can't *we* ever get ahead"—
on the bum
              in the soup
(fish peddlers, Foreign Legionnaires),
battling against the odds to keep odd jobs,
say "Easy Come, Easy Go,"
slipping a bull fiddle to a Pullman berth,
hey, I was in the war, Mac—yeah, ya big "Beau Hunks,"
the race for their hats in the street's high wind,
politest before a fight—
                        what is it fulfills expectation?—
hearing the cuckoo march, we
anticipate
            the primness in Ollie's Danish pastry fingers
testing the tip of a punched nose,
the miffed wince when cops call him, "Fatty," say
        "move along, Fatty,"
the fluttered tie and tiny smile, the helpless
"why don't you do something to *help* me?" or
"here's another nice mess . . . ,"

know
Stanley's shovel-footed gait, half-moon grin,
in danger of falling
asleep, telling the truth—"don't you *dare*
touch that ladder"—leaning
head on hand
to miss completely

II

but, in fact,
Laurel was the brains of the team,
cold, aloof, English,
a fierce woman-chaser, married eight times,
demanding always twice Hardy's salary,
while Babe,
who'd dance like a bear
for biscuits and honey,
thought (faint drawl and courtly manners)
his real life started at forty-five
                    when,
                        marrying,
he found untrue what he had believed for years—
no woman could love a fat, comic man

III

what is real?

Arthur Stanley Jefferson
                    and Norvell Hardy?

these two and their two roles make four
and those four one where
playing his opposite each
defeats the other

                    close your eyes—
there is the light-involving frame full
of a motion that is like music, discontinuous
yet finding its continuity in us, frame
supplanting, unmaking frame as note
displaces note
in movements of ablative grace

                                we
are the dark interpreters of the lighted square,
taught to see two dimensions as three, taught
to feel depth as time and time as depth,
the music plays itself out in us

O
melodic and relentless demolition—
ties clipped, pants ripped—who falls
through the chimney to the basement
bringing the house down with him yelling
"wohoohohoo oн!" and sits
till the last brick drops "pock"
on his head—
               to be
what it is about,
                    to be used up

these lives are the self-dissolving counterpoint
the music plays itself out in us

IV

that Ollie spent his last three years in a wheelchair,
paralyzed, unable to speak, the aristocratic
acrobat's lightness gone, light
dying on a coarsened face,
that Stanley and his last wife tried to live
in a beachfront apartment (dingy
with the bright sunlight of Santa Monica)
on a monthly government check
proves only
true lives are lived
                    moment to moment
by those
helpless to settle accounts
or save
        money,
                themselves, since these
end
    with nothing,
                  or very little,
beyond the perfected gesture
                            and the stance

what is true? suppose
someone says, what is true?

say,
    the truth is time
devours his sons,
and say,
each moment slays the one before,
its father,
and in turn, is slain

Song: The Musical Solution

The fulfillment dissolves the figure.
NORMAN O. BROWN

Pater said it,
All art aspires to take
The form of music and
Yeats did.

Mad Nietzsche wrote
Of tragedy music-born.
Hart Crane
Leaped to the caverned sea.

By senseless words
The child becomes his song:
An Apollonian dream
In waves undreamt.

Hopkins in secret
Broke the law of sense,
Fusing sensed objects in
Dionysian music.

Flawing one container
Shatters
Each—matter and form,
Body turned to soul.

Stevens thought
Our spirits make a music.
Yeats believed
The dancer trusts the tune.

But Eliot
Remarked a music felt
So deep we are
That liquid while it lasts.

Is it that poems
Speak their meaning or
Do what they are? In song,
What solitary thing is solved?

Glenn Miller

I

the black disc shunts sideways
                        drops   the hooked
arm lurches   locking
                  descends
catches the spiral track toward the center   that
inner empty space   the zero point no point
can ever reach
               within
which all revolves   the origin of sound

the opening notes of *Tuxedo Junction—*
if there are perfect things   then this is perfect
                            revenge
for growing up in Colorado
                    because
". . . from the stage of the Paramount Theatre"
                          the band
in summer tuxs   a blue spotlight   Glenn
in a white suit   maroon tie   the red
carnation   the rimless glasses   a bright gold trombone
                            "well
fellas and gals   here's the one you've been waitin for"
cue   (the brass muted)

doo-wát-doo-wah/one-twó-three-four/doo-wát-doo-wah/
    one-twó-three-four
doo-wát-doo-wah/one-twó-three-four/BOO———WAAH———/
    BOO———WAAH———
det-dunt-duh——/doo-wát-doo-wah/det-dunt-duh——/
    doo-wát-doo-wah
det-dunt-duh——/doo-wát-doo-wah/doo-wát-doo-wah/boo-wah

Marion Hutton last fall:
                    "I was heartbroken
                                        Glenn
was like a father   I never knew why
he gave me all those crap songs to sing   he just
liked Ray better than he did me"
seventeen when she joined the band   Glenn
was her legal guardian
when she sang Al Klink explained "troops,
the microphone is out of tune tonight"   Glenn: "we'll
cover up her singing with good arrangements"
Billy Finegan: "*her* singing   hell
I had to write them to cover his trombone
he played so loud he threw the brass out"

Glenn
        is smiling at the kids in the front row
they go wild   somewhere in the balcony they're chanting
"Glenn! Glenn!"
                    but he won't solo
("just remember, pal—you're no Tommy Dorsey")
                                            ever since
Jack Teagarden   replaced him with the Pollack band that
fierce deep need to be the best jazz trombone has been
the desire   just to have his own band   be respected
and to succeed   "we'll
make it on good arrangements
I'm sick of prima donnas"

now the hits are coming one on one

Adios   String of Pearls   At Last   In the Mood

"one of the best of a swell crop of new tunes is
This Time the Dream's on Me   here's Ray to sing it for you"

Serenade in Blue   Blue Moonlight   It's a Blue World
last chorus   the derby mutes
the trombones swinging left right left   the trumpets
upanddown   the saxes   (diagonally)
back and forth the band

                              rocking slowly in the light
the crowd poised in darkness

                                     like an animal holding its breath
he has always had this deep fear   like a dream   it *is* a dream
if he lets the music stop if he loses control of time
time will eat him up

("to succeed

                I just want to be a success")

people thought he got that drill with the mutes
from Lunceford

                  not knowing

                              he was born in Iowa   not
believing he'd lived in a sod hut   not
seeing   this was a small town drill team
a high school band

                  that played all its marches sitting down
"he was the General MacArthur of the business   Glenn
always cared more about discipline than music"
Johnny Desmond: "I was scared stiff of him   sometimes
he could be the nicest guy in the world   then   next minute

cold as ice   he made me feel like one of those kids
whose father doesn't love him   or never shows he does"
after the war, Billy May wrote Al Klink: "say,
did I ever tell you that Adolph Hitler is alive
and playing fender bass with Glenn
                                        in Argentina"

II

the couple in *American Gothic* were Glenn's parents
when he left to play trombone
                                they quarreled
". . . but a musician . . . Glenn . . .   is that respectable?"
they didn't understand   (why,   it's like a movie)
when he became a success
                        he bought them a new home   because
what else
            does any authentic success
                                        do to his father?

so Glenn   commissioned the mythic painting *American Classic*
a tux   instead of overalls and a black coat
a trombone in place of a pitchfork   the open frank expression
but the glasses are the same   Marion
standing beside him   the look on her face
empty as a field of wheat
she is holding a Coke   Glenn
is smoking a Chesterfield   behind
a green lawn   a white mansion   and a black
1940 Buick
                since

if this is sentiment
                    it is all chrome plate
                                        and black enamel
since
          it is endearing and American
                                        in that
simplicity and earnest grace
                    of a cheerleader
                                        or a majorette
because those who never understood said
his music was without emotion
                              never thinking
that something very beautiful without emotion's
                                        an emotion in itself
an American emotion
                         since this
                              precision
                                        almost erotic
defines the invisible thrill
                         of perfect revenge
because I never knew anyone who was any good
anyone who did his homework at the kitchen table as a kid
listening to New York on the radio who didn't know
when he heard the start of *Moonlight Serenade*
                                        exactly what it meant
"our second national anthem"

Sun Valley Jump   Skylark   Perfidia

Glenn: "we scored five saxes   clarinet lead
                                   Willie Schwartz

played it like an alto   what you recognized
was like a voice   but not a voice   it was voicing
it never was a voice"
                            because
if there are perfect things
                                    that way
of phrasing a line
                    and holding a note
                                        is perfect
revenge as technique

"you see   he thought if he praised a guy's work
the guy would ask for a raise
you know the type   right out of the middle west"

("to succeed
                just to be a success
                                            at least
not a failure like Pop")
                                ". . . since
both the babies were adopted
and Glenn
                never saw the little girl"

when his first band folded: "this time
no prima donnas   we'll make it on arrangements"

Glen Island Special   Little Brown Jug   Sliphorn Jive
Falling Leaves

"Tex was his favorite   and Trigger Alpert

they were like his sons   as far as I was concerned
he was a cold sonuvabitch   he told Jimmy Abato
he didn't want him in the band   because Italians and Jews
were troublemakers   said that   and you know his best friend
was Charlie Spivak   you figure him out
he was a type   right out of the middle west"

                                                    because
it is not ever
                    when you do
                                        what you have dreamed
but when you first
                            see   it can be done
and that it can be done by you
                                        before
you become
                    the captive of a name

III

finale   the audience is standing
                                            clapping
standing on the seats   cheering   starting
to lindy in the aisles
they won't stop   "you can't stop them!"   encore   "Glenn!
Glenn!"   they lap in waves around the stage
if he comes down front
                                he'll be swamped
the leader and his band   the actor
and chorus   his father's voice

Santa Fe Trail   Elmer's Tune   Slumber Song

because
              for us
                        there is only one city
"and now
                   from the Cafe Rouge of the Hotel Pennsylvania
Chesterfield brings you
Sunset Serenade
                        with Glenn Miller and his Orchestra"
it is a dream of the middle west
                                    the Big Apple
                                                      a late
autumn afternoon
                        banded with light and shadow
                                                            the tall
buildings in bright air
                        to be still young
                                          and a success
and in New York
                        now
                                    no going back
the war between
                        somewhere
                                    our only city was lost
". . . but it wasn't a voice   it was voicing
I wanted something that was good on paper   not
the sound of one instrument   not anything that needed a soloist
something that once it was written down
any good musician could play it and people would say

'that's Glenn Miller' "

Polka Dots and Moonbeams
                              When Johnny Comes Marching Home
The American Patrol

a voice on the air
"this is Glenn Miller saying
goodnight for Marion, Ray, and all the gang"

                                        since
to be an era means
                    finding a special way
of getting lost
                    so loss becomes
the space of an existence that
                              hole at the center
before and after
                    but never   here and now
to be a myth
                    a man must
                              vanish
                                        in the sky
                                             or in the sea
must
        become a melody
                              his body can nowhere be found
". . . when Glenn was lost in the war
                                   well   it was like
a symbol
        there was a whole world got lost with him

I have to laugh
            all this nostalgia
you know what Glenn planned to do when he got back?
move to California   ease himself out of the band business
                                                    be
the West Coast Coca-Cola distributor   Glenn   God love him"

Anvil Chorus   The Lamp Is Low   Juke Box Saturday Night

Chuck Goldstein of the Modernaires: "you hear lots of stories
I know   somehow the real Glenn gets lost
there were guys who hated him   I mean
really hated him   listen   when my father had a stroke Glenn
was waiting for me at the stage door
he'd already made the train reservations to Buffalo
I just got there
            an hour too late
I rejoined the band in Washington   after the last show
Glenn took me out to a club   he ordered a bottle of bourbon
and a bottle of rye and talked to me
until we got drunk   he was like a father   it was like
it had happened to him instead of me   they
can say what they want   in my book he was aces"

IV

"just wait   I'm going into this war
and I'm coming out some kind of hero"

when he walked off stage at the last show
he saw the band manager Johnny O'Leary
tears down his cheeks   an unlit cigar in his mouth

"O'Leary
          I hope I'm doing the right thing"
"I think you are, Glenn"

Omaha   to Fort Meade   to Maxwell Field
to Knollwood Field   to Atlantic City
to New Haven   and then
                              back on the air
theme   (voice over)
                      "Good evening, everyone,
this is Captain Glenn Miller with   *I Sustain the Wings*
brought to you by the Training Command
of the U.S. Army Air Forces. Tonight we're in Chicago
where we're lending a hand in the Fifth War Loan Drive
to keep those dollars moving to the fighting front.
We're broadcasting from the Service Men's Center
where already over twelve million men and women in uniform
have been guests of the city of Chicago.
Now let's get to a little music. Here are the boys
with their rocket-gun version of
                              Flying Home."

and then

          overseas

"the thing was   Glenn didn't hafta go
he was overage   he was married
the band was making almost a million dollars a year   he just
turned his back and walked away   patriotism my ass
what I think is   he never really believed in his success
he useta talk about the Miller luck   how it had lasted five years

how that was all anyone could expect
he just wanted to quit it before it quit him
that way afterwards he could say   'it was the war' "

Mission to Moscow   Saint Louis Blues March   Tail-End Charlie

                                                   that
hundredth time he couldn't get ice water in a restaurant
and blew up at the waiter   or when
the buzz bomb flattened the building where the band was staying
a day after they'd left   when
the sinus trouble came back and the colds he couldn't shake
when he started losing weight and the tailored uniforms
swallowed him up   the time
the band's plane almost went down
when he started losing at poker
(something he'd never done)   or when he threatened
to send half the band into the infantry
knowing
           the luck had quit
he told Haynes
               "I've known it for a long while   I'm
not coming back from this"
                     knew finally
                             what loss meant
and thought   "all right   just
let it be death
           and not failure"
                   knew
the finished work
          is a fragment

                                        ". . . voicing
it never was a voice"

"the thing was   Glenn didn't hafta go
he could've sent Haynes to Paris   that was his job
Glenn had a gift   it was real   look
there're people go into a new place first thing they do
is look for the exits   that was Glenn
over there in England he finally knew   it's
putting yourself in a place
                                        with no graceful way out"

sitting in the corner of a pub   writing to Helen
"everything's fine here
                                you know how much
I miss all of you
                                I'm hoping that we'll all be back
some time next fall"
                                lonely
                                        homesick
and now for the first time
                                        really afraid
he wrote to his lawyer
                                "just
let me come home
                                and *give* the government the taxes—
I don't care"

"this is the BBC London   bringing you recorded selections
played by Major Glenn Miller and his American Army Band
we begin with   *String of Pearls*"

"colonel
    I think we're wasting our time
                     even the birds are grounded"
"hold on, Glenn"
          the sound of the engine
                    muffled
closer
    and now
          past   "he can't find us"
sideslipping
      "just hold on"
            and then down   "hi
sorry I'm late   ran into some bad weather"
                "whaddaya call this?"
"relax, Glenn"
      "I'll see you tomorrow in Paris"
                "good luck"
"yeah
    we may need it
           hey
where the hell are the parachutes?"
      "what's the matter, Miller,
you want to live forever?
        get the door"
            pulling
his cap down tight   steps back
the plane
    lurches once
       taxis   starts
to turn

                    gaining speed
                              strains
                                        bouncing
                                                  once
                                                        twice
lifts

          and is gone
                              "listen, kid,   any man
who says his family's the most important thing in his life
is lying
              he just
knows he's a failure
so he's pretending
                        he really didn't want it—
like my Pop"

                    until
he has become a melody we know by heart
                                        and we
vanish in the rain and fog
                              in winter at night
flying across the channel
                              in the past   at war   so one
last thought   picture   image—
                              a white house
above a green lawn
                        two children in white summer clothes
running
              with open arms

                        where
the blue roadster
                  turns into the gravel drive—
takes our breath away
                           the plane
hits the blackness of water
                        and is gone

Circles

> Wherever an individual was of a mind to stand apart, to draw a circle of self-sufficiency about himself, philosophy was ready to isolate him still further, finally to destroy him through that isolation. NIETZSCHE

I

The Poet: Snapshots

> A photograph is a secret about a secret. The more it tells you, the less you know.
> DIANE ARBUS

Centering in photos:
Here he is at eight, crouched
Watching a horror picture,
    Set to heave with fright, when
Mom or Dad says,
"John, it's just a movie."
Somehow the frame's strait edge
    Makes the fear all right.

As if that alternative, quick
World where Adolph Hitler's
Nibelungen heroes
    Veered in steel despair
Could solve terrors that
Had clung to Lon and Bela
Boris and Peter Lorre, only
    Through a greater fear.

He hated school. This
Was snapped at recess when,
Waiting not to be picked
    For this team or that,

He made the double game
Where those who watch but can't
Be part replay it all in
    The mirror of pure thought.

That is a clarinet, that
A hand, a hand, a face,
Lost in the high school band,
    Tense *succès d'estime,*
Here forcibly being ejected,
Fighting to play at once all
The notes, fast and loud,
    All the time.

This was made at college:
Short hair, sincere, a huge
Bow tie for debate,
    (Can this be the right track?)
Last of the generation still
Taught to respect charm, dance,
Tell a joke, play
    The piano, do a trick.

In back is the ocean. That
Could be a deck, but
That would mean a ship so
    It's probably a dock,
The best traditions of the navy:
Sitting behind a desk, he
Coffees important papers and
    Watches a clock.

This next is a composite
Of all the girls he loved—
Taken in just that light its
    Indeterminate margin
Incorporates each new
Affront to the dream, much
The way Quixote believed
    Every whore a virgin.

He likes fast cars. That's
The first, low, sleek,
A beach, mountains beyond, his
    Back against the sun,
Young and special-seeming, but
The photo begins to fade to
Just a black outline and now
    Could be almost anyone.

Portraits of false starts,
A mirror, a mask, each fresh
Distortion in deep water,
    Who can distinguish the truth?
Doubt, a telescopic laugh, the last
Poise beyond these, that
Darkness in the eyes to
    The suddenness of the teeth.

Here he is at NASA
(*How to Steal the Moon*), forge,
Then force an all-consuming
    Circle yet with his

Sinecure in Houston as
(Phase eight, change two) at
The edge of a moving shadow, he
      Sits and wonders, "Whose?"

A table in a cellar and
A candle on the table, she (a gold
Seahorse at the collar, maroon
      Scarf, a blue dress),
He leans across and looks,
Stammers, upsets the wine, one
Image and its attention, say
      Yes, he says yes.

Reversed like a movie, here
Everything spirals backwards,
"Make it the way it was."
      He hears the music play.
How can words be real when
The dancers refuse to move?
His pictures are the music
      Cut up day to day.

Next shot: those are the sated
Children of the rich, that's
How to read a sonnet, this
      Who Hart Crane was, while
Here he suspends,
Willingly, disbelief, always
Keeping the leap of faith
      The last flop he does.

How long did he seek,
In gestures, in words,
A voice that commands no
        Matter the situation,
Convinces, persuades? And
Find it to say, "You
Should not have believed me.
        Art is dissolution."?

Here not so funny—
The change is that quick, too
Much work, much talk is what
        Wears the heart out, else
A picture has been lost, less
Deft, less intense from
Starting to bore his friends, he
        Starts to bore himself.

In this one he'll turn forty:
Staring at a mirror put
To steady his hand,
        Balding, ascetic,
Having seen a face so long
It scarcely makes sense his
Wondering how to meet
        The razor's distant nick.

He mimics the slashed picture of
An imaginary man
Spilling into song, even
        Gives the man a name

Whose slowbreaking makes a sense
Enjoyed for itself:
An arm bends from that picture,
    The hand points to the frame.

In this last he writes a poem, its
Non-voice to smash each
Mosaic of sound, word's
    Inward tumbling tower,
Self-created, compulsive,
He writes to negate the will,
Determined to play out
    The line that exhausts the power.

II

His Poem: Myth

Music and mythology confront man with virtual
objects whose shadow alone is real. LEVI-STRAUSS

    i

Richard Peredur and Kyre Cristinobyl met
In the garden of the Merveilleux Hotel,
Their phoenix love, an incendiary dance,
Beggared the weave of time and circumstance.
Eroded cheek and claw-like hand so tell
Their story yet to terrace, summer frock, and string quartet.
Roadsters of that fashion no longer wheel
Down roads above the sea. A scarf as blue and pale

I have not seen. Memory may fail.
It is all changed much in the telling, where once, it was all real.

    ii

The scene is of a Mabinogion played
By lacquered men, by dark-haired girls in cars,
Chromed and louvred, at the Paris or the Horseshoe Bars
Or the Plaza Palm Court fronded like a glade.
Here, a quarter past nineteen twenty-five,
In that first mist of manhood and of girldom,
To the clink of ice cubes tapped in tall cool drinks,
Dark Arabella dances what she thinks,
Her dream a dance, the dance a time-devouring dream.

                                          Boredom,

Gathering like bruised clouds on the *forêt des fauves*,
Let them play at who's the bravest, who's the fairest,
For Richard and Kyre, communioned, sit apart,
Bewildering the wheels and cylinders of the heart
Before the wordless descent from the terrace.

    iii

They are up above in the light,
I am below, waiting in the black garden.
Past the terrace   night is a cube crossed
By searchlights fencing to a music,
Close up   a dance of shadows
Lost, recast
Where Richard and Kyre move to one low note,
Drawn wordless to the dark   she laughs